A BOWL FULL OF BLESSINGS

A Sabbatical Memoir
Author: Dr. Sally A. Baas

A Bowl Full of Blessings

A Sabbatical Memoir

Author: Dr. Sally A. Baas

ISBN 978-0-9893405-8-8

Library of Congress Control Number: 2019938157

Publisher: How 2 Creative Services, 17550 200th Street, Audubon, MN 56511

Layout and design: Copyright © 2019, How 2 Creative Services of Audubon, MN

Consultant: Sarah How, School Psychologist

Cover artwork created by Wangsi Xiang and used with permission.

Original photographs provided by Author Dr. Sally A. Baas and used with permission.

A Bowl Full of Blessings… **A Sabbatical Memoir**

By Dr. Sally A. Baas

Dedication:

For my worldwide family –
I use my heart as my pen, my emotions as my ink,
my life as the paper upon which God charts my path … to cross with yours.

No human can paint the picture of your life. I know I haven't painted my own life's picture. God has handed me the brush, but he has created the masterpiece. He has painted my life's portrait filled with colorful people, colorful experiences, and colorful opportunities. I am so blessed, in fact, because my life is like a bowl full of blessings, crafted by the potter's hand.

The opportunities and the stories included here are like a bowl full of blessing piled high through months of meeting faculty, leaders and students, reading, reflecting, researching, and teaching at Huaihua University. It is told in both first and third person. The deep relationships have become the golden threads woven into the tapestry of this effort to construct a proverbial wind and rain bridge building friendships and community critical to teaching, research, learning and exchange. Most of all, we have created something called people to people diplomacy or citizen to citizen exchange which complements traditional diplomacy helping colleagues, both in China and America, to become acquainted. We are creating an exchange between two universities that will honor both and enhance the learning for all.

CONTENTS

JOURNEY

It has been said that a journey begins with a single step forward. This sabbatical journey on which I have embarked began simply that way… by stepping out and forward, offering to be a part of a new venture at our university to bring Chinese students and faculty to Concordia University, St. Paul, MN. In exchange we hope to send our students and faculty across 6000+ miles by air, bullet train, and car to Huaihua University, in Huaihua City. Huaihua is pronounced in English something like "Why-wha". Located in the mountains of the Hunan Province of China, it is where bowls of food are super spicy; spring weather is steamy, and friendships accompanied by endless cups of tea are deep and rewarding.

Travel is the movement of people between distant geographical locations. Travel by foot, bicycle, automobile, train, boat, bus, airplane, cars and walking with or without luggage, one way or round trip. Travel can also include relatively short stays between successive movements, and all the way finding as Emily Dickinson said, "Where thou art, that, is home." Thou means ever so many things to me. It means where I am, where you are, where my family and new friends are, and where I feel closer to the foundations of my faith. That became my home for months at a time at the international hotel across from the Huaihua campus.

When one plans for a journey, one knows they may "lose their footing momentarily, but dare not lose oneself," as Soren Kierkkegaard has said. Traveling alone across the globe was all new to me. I had made several trips to places including Russia, Norway, Sweden, the Netherlands, Thailand, China, Brazil, Lithuania, Poland, United Kingdom, and Japan; however never alone, always in the company of someone else for me to follow. This journey would begin alone and end surrounded by forever friends.

When one considers taking a semester or year away from typical university duties, there are many considerations and difficult questions to answer. For me, I needed to put the programs I direct and the classes I teach in the hands of others. I have deep confidence in my colleagues and trust them explicitly. Yet, I knew from previous experiences taking time away from my responsibilities to fill other roles, it would be difficult to return, because I knew things would be different. Settling my head about being gone, I proposed a plan for a one semester time focused on building a proverbial bridge for our exchanges.

What follows are vignettes of people to people diplomacy or citizen to citizen exchange which complements traditional and formal diplomacy to help my colleagues, both in China and America to better become acquainted and for my university colleagues to experience through my eyes a look into life in the Hunan province of China at Huaihua University.

> **"**
>
> I use my heart as my pen, my emotions as my ink,
> my life as the paper upon which God charts my path ... to cross with yours.
>
> **"**

BOWLS OF CONNECTION

Years before I made this trip, God laid on my heart a scripture from I Chronicles 4: 9-14 (RSV) known as the Prayer of Jabez which I prayed for some time, asking God to expand my reach to people from around the world. Through a series of circumstances I was led to Concordia University, St. Paul, which resulted in my directing the Southeast Asian Teacher Licensure Program for almost two decades, working with students from around the world with the deep commitment to be teachers in Minnesota schools. In 2004, along with some of my Hmong Southeast Asian Teacher Program students created the Hmong Culture and Language Program which has helped Hmong and other Pre-School through 12 graders, families and community members preserve their culture and language through storytelling, gardening and the arts. Partnering with school districts, local agencies, businesses, foundations, and the dedication and persistence of the Nao Thao, Chao Vang, their families, the youth clan leaders and my own family, especially my husband Jim, we have served over 12,000 summer Building Cultural Bridges campers and year-around Saturday program for children and youth. We have been teaching reading, writing and speaking Hmong, creating traditional arts, playing historical-specific games and eating traditional foods like Hmong sausage and papaya salad.

"

Years before I made this trip, God laid on my heart a scripture...

"

AMERICAN MOM AND CHINESE DAUGHTER #1

Having the commitment to the Hmong led me to meet Sarah Bu, a Chinese visiting scholar to the Center for Hmong Studies, at Concordia University, St. Paul, in August of 2017. Like, Sarah Bu, many Chinese persons have English names which will be explained more later. Sarah is a lecturer at Huaihua University. She is Hmong or Chinese Miao (one of the 56 minority groups in China). She came through a grant from the Chinese Government to our campus to study about Hmong individuals, their history, language, culture, and to get a better picture of the history of her own people. Sarah Bu and I spent a great deal of time together. She attended and participated in my Human Diversity classes, cooked and shared her special spicy Chinese lunches with those eager to try the firey hot Hunan dishes. She became a part of our Baas family. One example: she came to our home in December, dressed in her stylish over-the-knee boots and leather skirt and join our family of girls (daughter Mandy and Granddaughter Gretel) and helped cut out and frost Christmas cookies, one of our family traditions.

With my support, and that of other faculty, including Dr. Paul Hillmer, oral historian of Hmong people, Sarah conducted research while she was at our university, looking at the social-emotional well-being of Hmong and other students at the university.

Because of our special relationship, she christened me her "American Mom", and thus she has become my Chinese daughter! She is a special blessing in my singing bowl of life, and I believe a proverbial bridge for me to receive the invitation to Huaihua University after Dr. Zhang Ling, Vice President of that university signed a Memorandum of Understanding in 2017, to begin conversations about an exchange program for faculty and students with Concordia, focusing on the Art and Design faculty. Bridging these two universities became my sabbatical focus May 2018.

> "
> She is a special blessing in my singing bowl of life
> "

JOURNEY, A NEW BOWL OF BLESSINGS

This was a new journey for me, a journey on behalf of two universities, physically alone, but supported by my university, family, and Huaihua to acquire the tickets and paperwork: passport, the letters of invitation from the Chinese Consulate, the inviting university, the detailed visa application, the travel and health insurance, the meeting with the physicians, and travel doctors, inoculations, medications, and more.

So much excitement, and so much anxiety about what was to come… what would be my role; how would I navigate knowing so few words of Chinese; who would help me find the plane, customs when I arrived in China, taxicabs, and the apartment or hotels. So many new things to learn so quickly. Yet, I knew I had one traveler who would guide me and care for me, and I found comfort in these three Bible verses which I quoted in my head over and over on my first trip to Huaihua:

… do not fear, for I am with you; do not be dismayed, for I am your God; I will strengthen you and help you; I will uphold you with my righteous right hand. (Is. 41:10)

Do not be anxious about anything, and in every situation by prayer and petition with thanksgiving, present your requests to God. And the peace of God, which transcends all understanding, will guard your heart and your mind in Christ Jesus. (Ph. 4: 6-7)

Love is patient, love is kind. It does not envy, it does boast. It is not proud. It does not dishonor others, it is not self-seeking, it is not easily angered, it keeps no record of wrongs. Love does not delight in evil but rejoices in the truth. It always protects, always trusts, always hopes, always, perseveres. And now, these three remain: faith, hope and love. But the greatest of these is love. (I Cor. 13:4-7, 10 NIV)

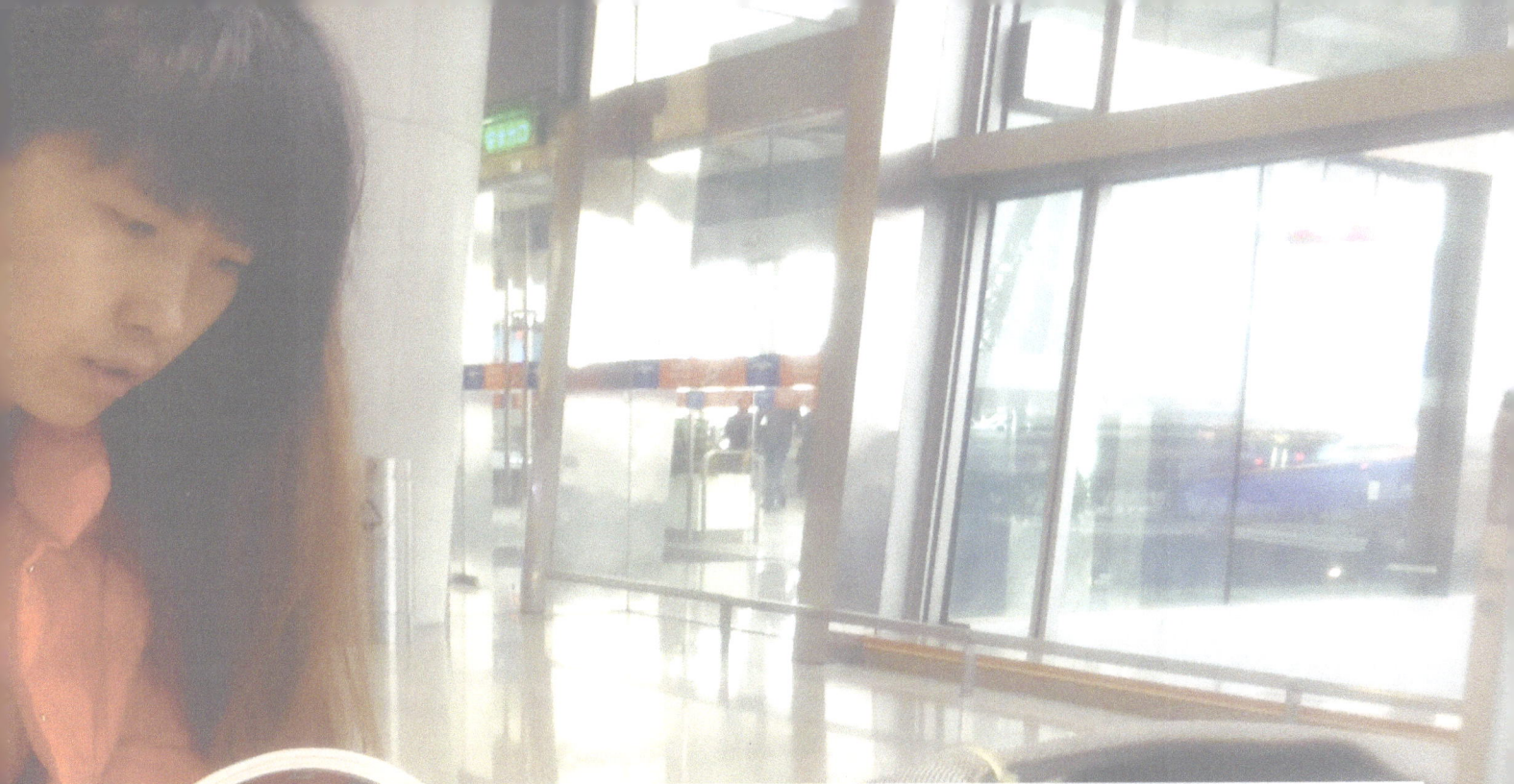

"

Do not be anxious about anything...

"

TRAVELING ANGELS

It is simply amazing the traveling angels who met me at every turn when I needed help and directions: a young man who said I looked like his mom (I thought he probably really meant grandma); a teacher from Vermont who was visiting her daughter in Shanghai; travelers from South Carolina and Kentucky whose warm Southern drawls were so comforting as they helped me move my luggage through Customs in the Shanghai Airport, blessing of the traveling angels.

Upon arriving in Changsha, at nearly midnight, seeing the welcoming sweet angelic face of Rachel on the other side of the baggage room gate, was more than I could have hoped for. Also, a driver to shuffle us off to a warm waiting car to take us to a friendly apartment for the rest of the few hours of the night. With a clean bed, but not towels and washcloths, I managed to clean up a little with something that looked like soap or shampoo, I fell into bed and right to sleep after setting my alarm. At 6:00 a.m., my phone rang, and I was greeted by a more than welcome kind voice of our son Brad who had called to be sure I had arrived safely in China. It was so comforting to have the joy of connection with the familiar and the faith I had arrived safely. Surely this is an example of the love that is shared by family and friends… what a blessing.

As the morning awoke, it was time to have some hot noodles and head for the high speed train to Huaihua, only an hour and fifty minutes, traveling at 300 kilometers per hour… what smooth speed as the train glided across the silvery rails through the deep green countryside of Hunan with its small villages, farms and gorgeous lush and velvety greens of all hues. I am amazed by the way all the trees are so close together, making it look like one green blanket on the mountains.

"

Surely this is an example of the love that is shared by family and friends… what a blessing.

"

THE BEAUTY OF HUNAN

I need to say a tad about the green of the mountains sliding by the windows of the train. The foliage is jammed so closely together that it looks like the rippling velvet of a little girls deep green Christmas dress. The streams and rivers that glimmer are like the satin ribbons trailing down from peaks invisible to the rider, yet like the flowing bows of a toddler running down the aisle of a sanctuary or orchestra hall. Never having seen such a carpet of inter-twining green vegetation.

On the train, people were snuggled into their seats taking rest while the train sped along at nearly 300 kilometers per hour. Blessed babies cuddled with their mamas while they gently sang lullabies to them while daddies looked on. Luggage was piled at the front of the train car, and packages hung on hooks by each seat or were stuffed overhead. At each small town, the train came smoothly to a stop and passengers quickly traded places, some onto the platform and others sliding into the open seats left by other passengers. Quickly people settled in, and the train was smoothly on its way to the next village stop. About an hour and a half passed, and the Huaihua station was announced over the loud speaker, and Rachel and I struggled through the crowed walkway to wrestle my two suitcases to the door. As soon as the door slid open, we drug them off the train and on to the waiting walkway. Again another angel, a university car driver met us and hoisted my bags into the car. Honestly, I don't think they were too happy I had such heavy bags full of clothes and gifts, but they said nothing (at least to me), and merely pushed and tugged to make them fit into the trunk which barely held the two big bags. At that moment, I was pledging to myself that next time, I wouldn't bring so many things! If only that would have held true. More about that later.

"
Never having seen such a carpet of inter-twining green vegetation.
"

HUAIHUA AND UNFORGETABLE WELCOME.

After we reached Huaihua, we drove about 30 minutes. I was warmly greeted by the Huaihua University faculty at my hotel room where there were armloads of gorgeous flowers, fruit, treats, and many friendly faces and warm hugs from all. The hospitality is more than generous. What a pleasant welcome!! We were quickly scurried off for lunch on the second floor of the hotel. It was like a 10 course meal with dishes of pork and peppers, beef and ginger, chopped pickled radish, egg custard, tofu with chicken and peppers, duck, eggplant, goose, scrambled eggs with tomatoes, and fish soup. There I had my first experience with chopsticks. Hum, that was my first real challenge. I asked for a fork and spoon amid raised eyebrows, and I realized that was not a good choice. Several days later, I came to better understand T.S. Elliot's quote about persistence, "If you aren't in over your head, how do you know how tall you are?" I routinely felt over my head in many ways, but over the weeks I was in Huaihua, I recognized that I must make changes in the way I do things that seem at first difficult, but are accomplished with perseverance. As the weeks flew by, I became rather accomplished with chopsticks and eating fish with bones. No doubt, I was vulnerable to the culture and skills of others, giving me opportunities to learn about myself and my desire to please others and build my capacity.

Next came meeting faculty and soon to be friends and to enjoy the beauty of my Chinese home so far away from the security of what I know best in Minnesota. My new home was filled with gorgeous bouquets of flowers, plates of delicious fruit, and delicious tea, plus bags of figs, nuts, chestnuts and all I could want or need for my comfort in Huaihua. Dr. Zhang Ling, Vice President of Huaihua came for frequent visits when I first arrived to assure me that we had lots of work to do ahead, and I would be doing translation and teaching while I was there. Translation meant, I would take materials already translated from Mandarin Chinese to English, and my role would be to translate (or edit) them into Academic English, so they would be ready for publication in the United States.

Very soon I was introduced to Angela Chung, my translator who would accompany me everywhere on campus and beyond, because there were few English speakers there except for those teaching in the School of Foreign Language.

> **"**
>
> The hospitality is more than generous. What a pleasant welcome!!
>
> **"**

AMERICAN MOM AND CHINESE DAUGHTER/TRANSLATOR #2

My anxiety about not knowing Chinese was very quickly alleviated by Angela, my first translator, a graduating senior who took me on as her project to meet my every need while I was at Huaihua, and continues to be by Chinese daughter today. Angela and I clicked from the moment we met. This big- brown-eyed young lady who was studying to be a teacher, had from all her growing up years been the mother figure in her home with no mother for a model, she created her own role to care for her father in every way by cooking, cleaning, and making a good home for him. All those skills carried over to her ability to help her colleagues in the group she mentored at high school and in college, and to being completely focused on me being safe and successful at Huaihua. She saw ahead of my needs for things including meals, treats, beverages and all. She even saw to it that my bottled water caps were loosened when I couldn't do it myself. Whenever there was a concern of any kind, she was there to meet my needs. Her translations were thorough, including helping me understand the side conversations and jokes that I would never have understood. She even bought me nylons when I ran out of my own. A side note- Chinese nylons are the very best I have ever found in the world! They almost never run. Sometimes you have to go across the world to find just what you need, and have always wanted!

Perhaps because of Angela's background and not having seen her mom for many years, she called me her "American Mom," and has to this day remained a very special part of our extended family. She is has been teaching Pre-K-1-2-3 graders in the Philippines and will be moving on to complete her Master's Degree soon. I am sure her students love her, because on Teacher's Day they recognized her with more gifts than any other teacher. I can certainly understand their admiration.

When she left to go home to see her father before going to the Philippines to teach, we had an emotional goodbye, yet hoping to see one another again sometime. And that came to be not long afterward when I was leaving Huaihua for the U.S. We met briefly again in Changsha as my train arrived there and she also arrived there by bus. She was waiting on the other side of the gate when I got off the train. She was standing there with arms wide open welcoming me to Changsha. We hugged forever it seemed, and then went to the Kentucky Fried Chicken restaurant for an ice cream cone. I met her sister who had accompanied her, and introduced her to Echo, my new translator, who had accompanied me on the train. It was really a difficult time saying goodbye again as she went to board the plane for Manilla.

We still keep in touch by sending messages and pictures by WeChat, hoping someday to connect in person again, American Mom and Chinese daughter #2. She hears with her ears, sees with her eyes and connects with her heart. Knowing her is like the chili in my bowl of noodles, such a flavorful spark of life!

Back to life in Huaihua…

> **She hears with her ears, sees with her eyes and connects with her heart. Knowing her is like the chili in my bowl of noodles, such a flavorful spark of life!**

"IT'S A SMALL WORLD, AFTER ALL."

"It's a world of laughter, a world of tears. It's a world of hopes, and a world of fears. There's so much that we share, that it's time we're aware. It's a small world after all."

These words from the Disney tune by Richard M. and Robert B. Sherman spin in my head as I see the "air-cleaning" truck playing the tune on a loud speaker as it rumbles by my window., Twelve stories below my room it is shooting steam into the air four or five times a day. God seems to be reminding me that China is a big, big country, and Huaihua City is but a small village of 200,000 people with a university bulging with 20,000 students tucked into this beautiful mountainous region of Southern China. It is a small world after all, and I have been called here to hear that song, to be reminded of my personal purpose to keep children, youth and families in the palm of my hand, as I focus positively and proactively to habitually seek God's plan. For through Him, I am able to follow his path to be a connector for those with needs while also seeking to find new ways to build their inner strength and capacity as learners.

In my quiet room in the Huangzu Hotel, on Jinhai Road, in Huaihua, I have had the privilege of editing the book *Natural Arrival*, written by Liu Kebang (2018), a Hunan financier. His essays tell the stories of a man dedicated to his family, his country, and his Party. I have had the opportunity to reflect on a piece of his writing (2018, p. 145), which clearly speaks to my life's goals and purpose of being a bridge to connect people together to meet the needs of others. Here a child asks

"My dear Priest. You have a clear idea of Heaven. Please tell me what Heaven is and what Hell is." The priest did not reply to his question directly but said, "I would like to take you to a place and have a look, and then I will tell you." The child was puzzled, and followed the priest to the place. Looking up, they saw a grand hall. A large table was placed in the central hall, and on the table were rich foods such as chicken, duck, fish, meat, and so on. The priest told the child, "This is Hell." The child asked the priest dubiously, "Life in Hell is not any worse than in our world. It is not as tragic as I might have imagined."

The priest said, "Don't worry. Please wait and see." A few minutes later, it was time for dinner and the door was opened. Hungry ghosts with shabby clothes, disheveled hair, and dirty faces, looking thin like walking skeletons came in succession, and pushed and pulled to try to take the food from the table. But in front of them was a pair of three-foot long chopsticks. They tried every means to use the chopsticks to get the dishes. But the chopsticks were so long that none of them could reach the food. The child said, "It is too miserable. How could they be treated like that?"

"They are suffering the temptation of food, but they cannot eat." The priest said. "Do you really think it is miserable? Let's go to another place.

"In heaven, the situation was the same. Delicious food was placed on the table and each person was given a pair of three-foot long chopsticks. By contrast, the people around the table were lovely. They used the same chopsticks. They lived together in peace and helped each other. You put the food into my mouth, and I put the food into your mouth. They cooperated very well, feeding each other and sharing the delicious food. Everyone was eating happily. It was obvious that human beings created the difference between Heaven and Hell.

Yes, this is a terribly striking illustration. Yet, it has made me think even more about how important it is for people to work together, to succeed together, and to meet the needs of others together.

I reflect and contemplate how do I add value to others? Questions that tug at me: What do I cry about? What do I sing about? What do I dream about?

> **For through Him, I am able to follow his path to be a connector for those with needs while also seeking to find new ways to build their inner strength and capacity as learners.**

LOST IN TRANSLATION

So much communication, so few words in Chinese, so much to learn, and for example, even though I watch carefully while others eat their noodles, I sometimes struggle with getting the breakfast noodles wound sufficiently around my chopsticks or the peanuts slide out of my grasp. It reminds me of all the things that God directs in my life, and how twisted and wound together are the strands of decisions which are sometimes difficult to sort out, especially without clear communication. It also reminds me of how dependent I am on God's meeting my small and seemingly insignificant things in my life, because he helps me with even these little things like peanuts and noodles.

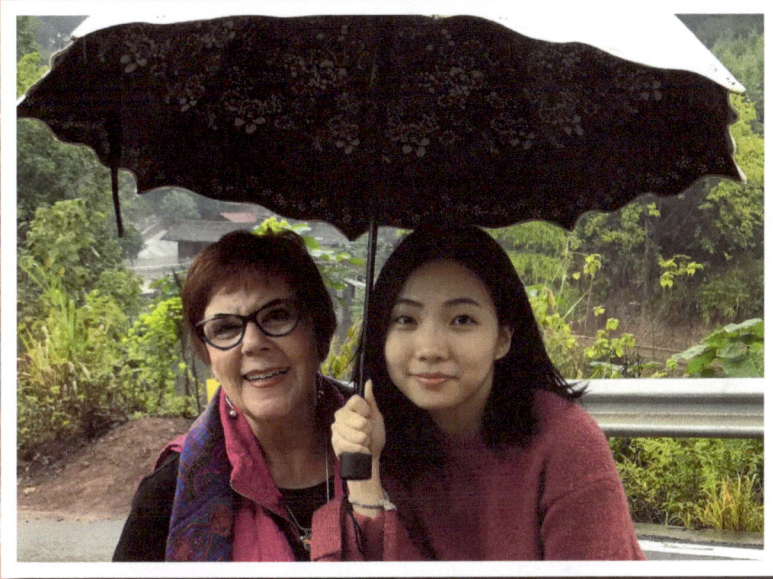

> "
>
> So much communication, so few words in Chinese, so much to learn, and realizing all the time so much is lost in translation, but also I have learned that when you don't have language, you have to watch, being always a keen observer.
>
> "

ESL CLASS AND HAPPY BIRTHDAY

During the spring, I was teaching English as a Second Language Methods class with Dr. Zhang Ling, focused on guiding the pre-service teachers to help their future students think critically by using ideas which included things like helping students slow the pace of teaching, helping students understand other's viewpoints, role playing and hitchhiking on others ideas, somethings they hadn't yet explored.

On one particular day, our lesson was to teach about American birthdays, so following the provided curriculum, we explored the tradition of cake, congratulation cards, and singing "Happy Birthday to You." As we finished, I surprised my students with the Chinese version of birthday cupcakes delivered to our class by the local baker. My students were so surprised, as they reported they hadn't had treats provided by their teacher in class before. So, I learned more about their context, and they learned more about traditions from my growing up years. It was especially fun for me, because it was my real birthday, and my first time celebrating in China. Later in the day I had lunch with my translators and dinner with teaching colleagues, a special day indeed.

> "
> Woven through every moment of every day are the golden threads of the working relationship and friendship that beautifies and strengthens.
> "

RELATIONSHIPS

Woven through every moment of every day are the golden threads of the working relationship and friendship that beautifies and strengthens what is being constructed between Concordia University, St. Paul and Huaihua University. It is being designed and constructed like a Chinese American tapestry. I feel a bit like a needle carrying the thread. Through my eyes, I see the beauty that is being created, yet am so aware of the knots that lay under the surface of the cloth. Some of the knotty things to work through are entry requirements for students – must pass the Tofel English tests, the HSK5, level 3 Chinese portion, weigh the articulation agreements, the course descriptions, the completion and graduation with all the requirements met. There is much complicated paperwork for content schools, universities, state, provincial, national and governmental regulations to sort through, yet, the beauty of the golden thread of relationships is what will ease the knots and make the upside of the tapestry of a collegial opportunity for students to study across the vast sea with opportunities to learn about art and design from unique perspectives.

> **"**
>
> Woven through every moment of every day are the golden threads of the working relationship and friendship that beautifies and strengthen.
>
> **"**

SHARING ART AND DESIGN

More and more I am building relationships with faculty and students at Huaihua, sending photos to Concordia of the art faculty, the art and design products, and the student art and design space at Huaihua to help to inform the CSP Art and Design faculty with whom we are building the cooperative learning opportunities. And, of course, I was learning about Huaihua University's location, the surrounding communities, the local Dong villages, and how to navigate the four lane road that separates the university from the hotel… no small thing to cross safely many times a day to the canteen to eat, to class, and to take long walks around the track at the Physical Education building and playground.

From my window, as I write, I hear the soulful sound of the gourd flute as the player uses his artistic musical skills to waken the morning, and assure me that peace prevails. It so reminds me of this scripture from Ps. 28:7(NIV) "The Lord is my strength and my shield. My heart has trusted in him, and I am helped. Therefore, my heart greatly rejoices. With my song I will thank Him."

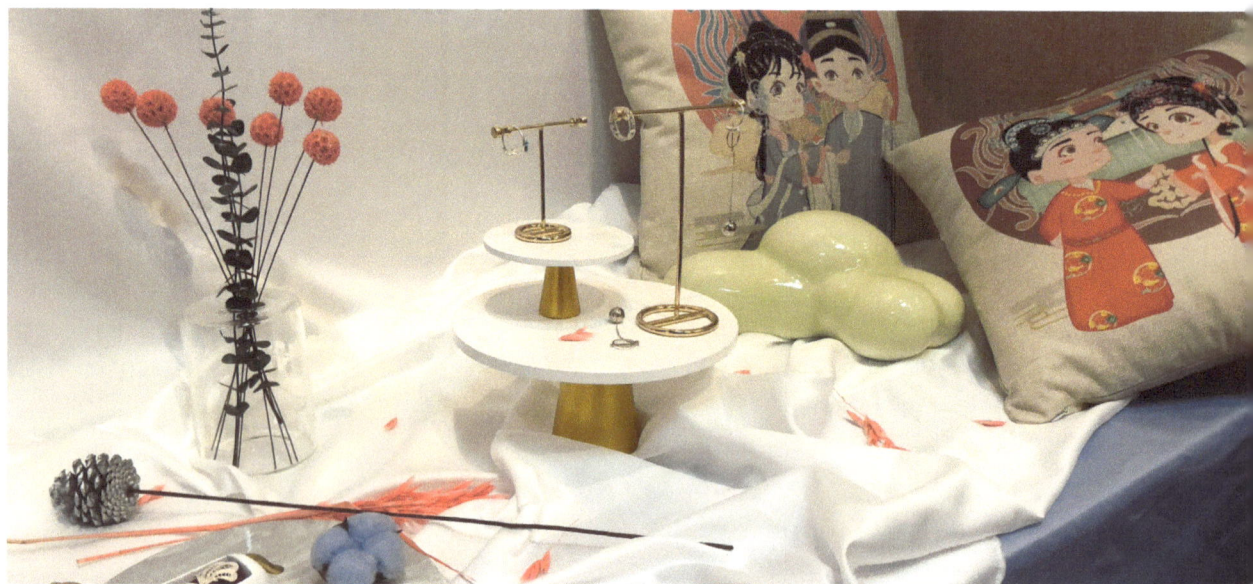

"

From my window, as I write, I hear the soulful sound of the gourd flute as the player uses his artistic musical skills to waken the morning.

"

VISIT IN MINNESOTA, A JEWEL-COLORED TAPESTRY

Between two visits to China on my sabbatical there was a time in August when, much like a brilliant jewel-colored tapestry, was the bringing together of the Art and Design faculties of the two universities in St. Paul MN. It was a time when the tapestry of this exchange had many ideological intertwining threads crisscrossing under the final product. During 11 summery days on the Concordia University, St. Paul CSP) campus, Huaihua University and Concordia University, St. Paul individuals studied, toured, and visited together. There was an interweaving of knowledge, skills, personalities, pedagogy, culture, good humor, and languages simultaneously bringing together more than 35 professionals with unique instructional and administrative skills focusing on enriching each other's teaching and making plans for future educational personnel and student exchanges.

I had sent home pictures of the artists' and designers' studios, classrooms, and workspaces to share with professors in St. Paul, MN, focused on helping Concordia faculty to visualize the settings where the professors and lecturers work at Huaihua University, and to build a foundation for the Chinese Art professors and designers to be ready for their two-week summer visit to America to learn about the Art and Design Program in St. Paul. That formed the foundation of conversations and work together.

> "
> There was an interweaving of knowledge, skills, personalities, pedagogy, culture, good humor, and languages simultaneously....
> ...now signing the MOU
> "

THE GOLDEN THREAD

The golden thread of relationships was woven through the tapestry of days together deepening our trust with each other. We have been professionals sharing our expertise, despite the language barriers which sometimes were intrusive to our full understanding. There was a commitment among the whole group to come to an agreement about how to create an articulation agreement for sharing courses and pedagogical methodology so students from each university may complete programs in art and design. Hours were spent by the Art and Design faculties on the articulation of individual classes led by John and Mandy, and overall coursework; yet, many details were yet to be finalized by Keith, Cate, Stephanie and Brad at CSP and all of the faculty from Huaihua. There is still much to learn for me, and for my Huaihua and St. Paul colleagues.

I am back to Huaihua and it is October in the beautiful mountains of Southern China, and I am so glad to be back with my friends there and looking forward to visits from friends from the United States and Australia. I hope they will like the food here, like spicy noodles.

> **"**
>
> The golden thread of relationships was woven through the tapestry of days together deepening our trust with each other.
>
> **"**

NOODLES

Noodles are for every meal. This province (Hunan) is known for its hot spicy noodles. Noodles for breakfast. Noodles for lunch. Noodles for dinner. Noodles for a snack. There is a noodle shop everywhere you go, and friends gather there to share the day's news, plan their weekend, work on their homework. It is much like a coffee shop, as you have the opportunity to order just your "cup of tea" so to speak—a little more cilantro, roasted peanuts, hot chili in oil, garlic, onion, pork with mustard greens, beef and garlic or fish and peppers. You can add green peppers, and anything you can think of to your noodles. My favorite breakfast noodle dish is cooked pork with fried mustard greens, some lettuce with cilantro, roasted peanuts, chili, garlic and onion… a great way to start the day! Of course, getting the last drop of the broth is only captured by tipping your bowl and slurping it up, trying not to spill on your new Chinese jacket.

A bowl of noodles each morning was my staple breakfast. Even though I watched carefully while others ate their noodles, I sometimes struggled with getting the breakfast noodles wound sufficiently around my chopsticks, the veggies and fried egg which wanted to slide out of my grasp, also like capturing the peanuts one at a time to pop into my mouth. These struggles reminded me of all the things that God directs in my life, and how twisted and wound together are the strands of decisions which are sometimes difficult to sort out, especially without clear communication. It also reminds me of how dependent I am on God's meeting my small and seemingly insignificant needs in my life, because He helps me with even these little things like peanuts and noodles.

> "
> It also reminds me of how dependent I am on God's meeting my small and seemingly insignificant needs in my life…
> "

ENGLISH NAMES

As you can imagine learning all the complicated Chinese names of my colleagues and students was looking like a yeoman's job, and I was so concerned about how I would accomplish it, especially remembering that their surname always comes before their given name, until I learned that due to the phone platform WeChat, nearly everyone has an English name. Of course, because of their lack of knowledge about American names, some of the names are somewhat unique like Cream, Calf, and Queenie.

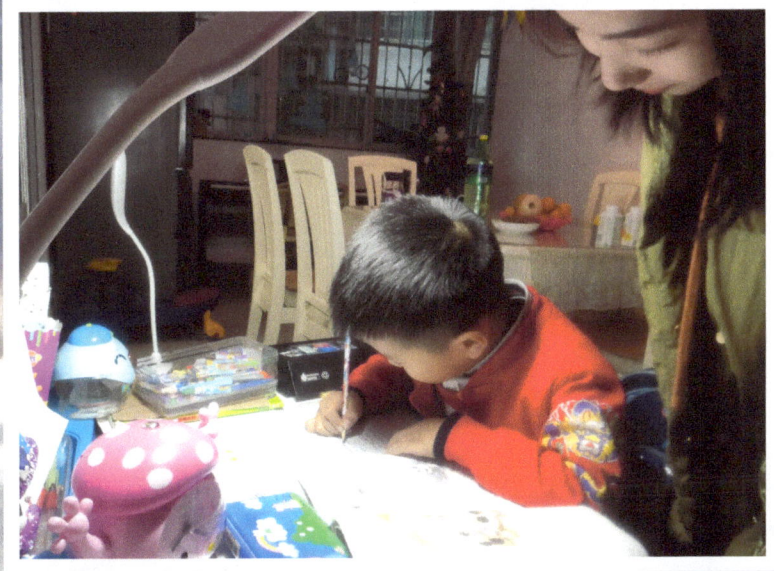

> "
> ...until I learned that due to the phone platform WeChat, nearly everyone has an English name
> "

UMBRELLAS, UMBRELLAS, UMBRELLAS

Umbrellas. umbrellas, umbrellas. "A cluster of dark clouds gathered in the sky. And the cluster, like a naughty boy drew back his bulging packet and mischievously poured water in large drops on the earth," spoke Liu Kebang (p. 37) This is nearly an everyday occurrence in Huaihua, so everyone carries an umbrella almost always. Umbrellas are everywhere in Huaihua, pink ones, blue plaid, green leaves, ones with fat cats, or black and white polka dots. You imagine the printed umbrellas, and you will see them almost every day… rain or shine, because they are lined with black to protect you from the hot sun, or keep the never-ending rain off. If you ride a motor bike, you have an umbrella that has a long tail of sorts that goes back over the persons riding with you, maybe a grandma, mom, baby, dad and a little toddler squeezed among you as you spin down Jujang Street between the Huangzu Hotel and Huaihua University campus. If you need to stop at the hotel to visit or to stay there, you are warmly greeted with a clear plastic bag for your precious umbrella, so it doesn't drip all over the meticulously clean ceramic tile of the entry way or leave a puddle in your room or the dining room where you are meeting friends for a late lunch. The plastic bag is not like the long ones you see in the United States that hold a yard tall umbrella like you use at the football game, but a foldable umbrella that has such a unique fold . It folds down and then folds outward looking like a cupcake liner for your birthday treat with the handle as the candle on your pretend cupcake. No one would dare venture outside any day without an umbrella.

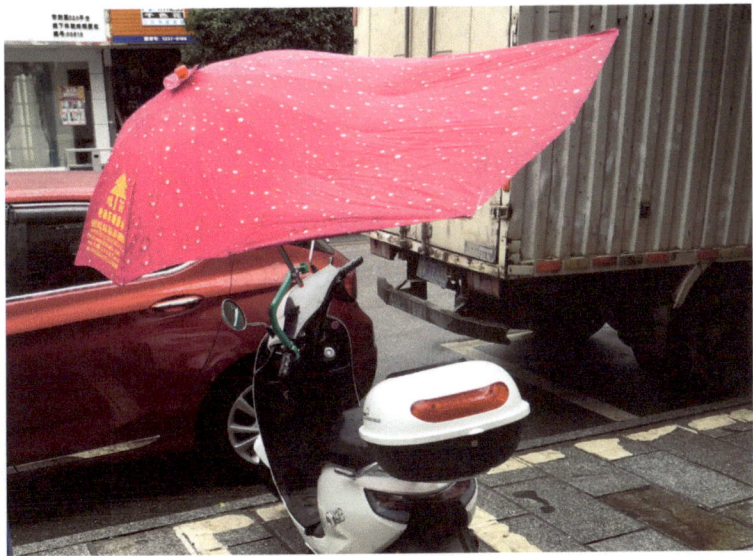

> "
>
> Umbrellas are everywhere in Huaihua, pink ones, blue plaid, green leaves, ones with fat cats, or black and white polka dots.
>
> "

VINYL SCREENS

Zooming around all the pedestrians, cars, trucks, trams, buses and moms and grandmas with darling little ones in plastic strollers, are those on aforementioned motorbikes. They, like the umbrellas, come in a myriad of colors, mostly red, but green, yellow, white, blue and a few purple ones, and about 90 % of them adorned with a vinyl screen wrapped not sideways, but over the front the handlebars and securely fastened behind the driver's seat to protect the driver from flying rain, leaves, mud, fumes and any other flying objects. When one is crossing the street, it is virtually impossible to know whether the driver is your friend or enemy, as you really cannot see who the person is… this always makes me wonder how they see who is in front of them as they buzz along darting around all the objects, people, and hand drawn carts of boiling hot food, freshly picked vegetables and fruit, plus the other modes of transportation filling the road with no vehicles really staying in any certain lane. Oh, of course, the screens are accompanied by the one or more umbrellas.

"

They, like the umbrellas, come in a myriad of colors…

"

INTERNET AND ELECTRICITY

Internet services are unpredictable. But, the electricity works like a charm if you put your hotel room entry card in the outlet holder. Of course, if you forget to take it out when you go to breakfast (which is nicely provided by the hotel), you are dead out of luck. You cannot get in the room or turn on the electricity for the lights, heat or air conditioner. However, the hotel staff is happy to have someone open your door if you have the proper identification with you, so never leave your room without your passport and ID.

插卡取电
Insert For Power

> "
>
> ..electricity works like a charm if you put your hotel room entry card in the outlet holder.
>
> "

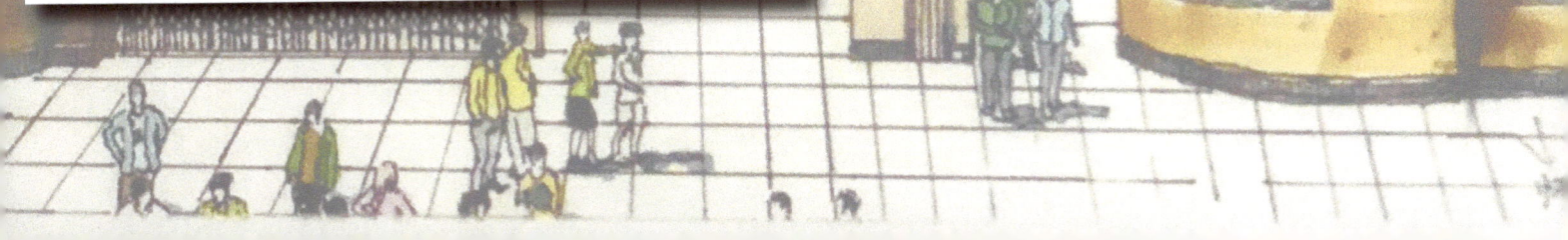

RAIN AND WIND BRIDGES

Visiting Southern China is a feast for the eyes, not only the people and the spectacular spicy food, but the sights of the rain and wind bridges which are built by the Dong people, one of the 56 minorities in China. The bridges are built with such a unique structure that you wouldn't want to miss a lovely day visiting one or more of these bridges. The closest one to Huaihua University is in Zhejiang, my personal favorite. Here the bridge not only allows safe passage across the river, but is home to many shopping attractions, such as new seasonal clothing, scarves, rain boots and shoes. There are food vendors and opportunities for the community, especially the elders, to gather to play Mahjong, the traditional three string violins, or just to sit and visit while watching the little ones making friends together sharing games and trinkets while eating steamed bread, pickled radishes, noodles, dried meats, corn on the cob, or caramel corn. Weary from shopping on the rain and wind bridge, tourists join in the fun as everyone gathers later at the nearby village center square for dancing in the evening. What a sight to see as the colored lights come on in the evening, lighted balloons with a variety of shapes and sizes reflect the relaxed atmosphere while the dancers, primarily women, exercise while they entertain the locals, who have likely been doing their laundry down at the rivers' edge where rubbing stones are available to scrub out the stains. Women laugh and sing with the joy of working together doing traditional tasks made more fun together.

> "
>
> Here the bridge not only allows safe passage across the river, but is home to many shopping attractions,...
>
> "

AM I JUST A WANDERER?

"Go from your country, your people, and your father's household to the land I will show you… I will bless you… and you will be a blessing." Genesis 12:1-2 (NIV)

Sometimes at night or early in the morning, I stare at the ceiling in my hotel room and then look out the window trying to make out the buildings through early morning fog. I think about how I have come to be in China and why am I here at this time and this place; and then, I get an email from a student, like today's:

"Thank you so much for giving me encouragement and understanding. I enjoy the time we spent, and I really like to spend more time with you if I don't have so many things to do. You always makes me feel warm, relaxed and happy just like my family. I learned a lot from you and you really are an amazing woman, knowledgeable teacher, as well as a kind friend for me. Sometimes I don't do my work well and it is not satisfactory, but you are willing to forgive and comfort me and move me. I am so sorry about my negligence that makes you feel bad, and I really appreciate your understanding. Sometimes I just cannot express to you how grateful I am. These days spent with you will be a happy memory for my whole life. Hope you enjoy all the following days in China and I will always miss you.

Thanks for your support and all the best wishes for me. I will try my best to perform well in the test and I also can be positive in the face of defeat because I don't think I do well in my preparation and review of my test and I still have to improve and progress a lot. It is a challenge as well as an opportunity to test myself from the prospective of my learning ability and anti-pressure ability. I always believe that It is because of all the things and all of you that I can be more mature, more elegant and smarter.

And I quickly responded:

"You also provide me great encouragement!! You are an amazing young woman and you are going to have great success in your life, for which I am very certain! Listen to your heart and it will guide you, always be true to yourself, with integrity strength and courage. It is my great privilege to know you and to have walked and talked with you… Blessings on your journey. I know that you will do well on your tests for graduation, and that you will be able to have a wonderful profession as you go forward in your life! You also, will be a wonderful memory for me!

It is in moments like these I knew I was in China for that moment in time to be an encouragement to a graduating senior that is rushing to completion of requirements, yet afraid of what lies ahead, the unknown.

Success is gritty, sweaty, and takes time. Sometimes you have to be released from something to be called to something else.

Letting go… a change of pace, a change of place, a change of perspective. At times our best efforts are not good enough to meet the high criteria, and we have to re-write, redo, re-edit, restructure our thinking, and re-submit our work again for real progress to begin. Liu Keback (p. 23), noted in his chapter on Tasting Life, "There should be more mutual understanding among people (student, teachers and families), which is the real yardstick of progress in a civilization." Or, just among people trying to make a difference in other's lives.

"

I think about how I have come to be in China and why am I here at this time and this place; and then,…

"

TRANSLATORS AND INTERPRETERS

Have you ever been in a place, a country, or an unfamiliar working place without the skills to communicate thoroughly for complete understanding? Let me tell you how it is for me… everything is **lost in translation**.

Without the assistance of a wonderful team of student translators: Queenie, Skye, and Bruce, Cream and Olia, and teacher translators like Echo, and interpreters like Rick at Huaihua University, I would never be able to understand all that is going on in a simple inter-change with colleagues, speakers, shopkeepers, or food vendors.

For example, one evening my translator Bruce asked me, "Do you square dance?"

I responded quickly with an oration of learning to square dance as a 6th grader in Mr. Ronald's class, and I jabbered on and on about the fun I had, "Of course I love to square dance…bowing to my partner and bowing to my corner. I love the step to the middle, stepping on out, and sashaying around the circle…" He looked so confused.

I asked, "What's wrong, Bruce??

He said, "I am talking about walking to the Huaihua City Square and dancing with all the students and the community people. I have no idea what you are talking about…" Let me check my phone translation… just a minute…" And then we had a really good laugh, as we realized we were merely **lost in translation**.

> "
> Have you ever been in a place,
> a country, or an unfamiliar
> working place without the skills
> to communicate thoroughly for
> complete understanding?
> "

THE THINKING CHAIR

It is still morning, and I am showered, dressed, and all. Time to sit in the Thinking Chair. No matter where I travel, I establish a Thinking Chair where I begin my day studying and reflecting.

Interesting, as I am sitting here thinking about teaching Emily Dickinson for the American Literature Class, I am thinking about her statement, "Where thou art, that is home." Here, in this Thinking Chair, I am home for seven weeks, here in China, a place I never in my life considered being for even one day, but God has plucked me out of St. Paul, MN, and put me here on the path he has created. It is a time of pause. My sabbatical is so different from what others have described for me. I am alone, yet in the middle of a university of 20,000 students in a village of 200,000 people. It's a small world after all. I think I am here to help make changes in how teachers teach and how students learn. However, as a trusted friend, Sarah, has said, "China must paint its own masterpiece."

From this thinking chair, I notice a white paper with one large dot, just a doodle really. I contemplate that large dot on a plain all-white page. It makes me think of me being here with so little experience in China. Am I the dot or am I the whiteness? If I am the dot, there is so much to see beyond this dot, so much world outside my window with needs, troubles, and on the other hand, so much laughter, joy and sweet experiences to be shared. What is my role here? I keep thinking… "In my blindness (of the whiteness around the dot), you are my vision, Lord"

The questions continue to tug at me about how can I add value to others? What do I cry about? What do I sing about? What do I dream about?

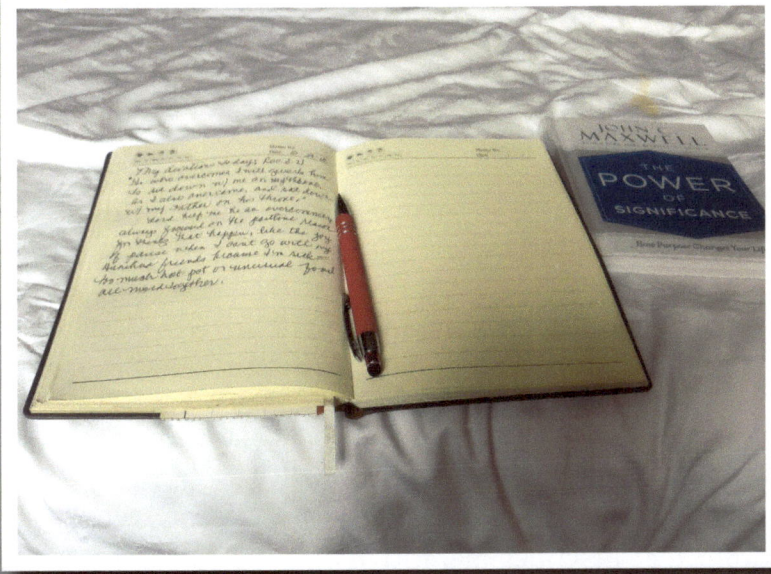

> "
>
> No matter where I travel, I establish a Thinking Chair where I begin my day studying and reflecting.
>
> "

THE SINGING DONG BOWL

Walking through a beautiful Dong village in October is such a sweet experience as the fall fruits are beginning to decorate the baskets at the small fruit stands… oranges, grapefruit, persimmons, dragon fruit, apples, pears, and more. As we strolled along with friends this sunny afternoon, we passed a small tea shop with lovely tea sets, but none for sale so we meandered on down the lane. Later after lunch, we were coming back past this same little shop and the potter was having tea with some friends in the shop. One of my Chinese colleagues, Lisa, stopped to chat with him. She is an oil painter-instructor at Huaihua. She inquired about the purchase of one of his tea sets and he led her and the rest of us who were there together that day- Handsome David, Queenie, Sarah, and Tim, to his green ware room where hundreds of tiny tea cups and tea pots of all sizes were drying. He invited Lisa to make her choice of items to be painted and fired to her desired color, etc.

As we were leaving the store, I commented about a bowl the potter/owner held in his hand, one made with local clay. The potter told us it had significant amounts of iron in the clay. When he flipped his thumb and middle fingernail against it, it made a lovely *dong sound*, like that of a mid-range bell. I exclaimed, "Wow, it sounds like 'DONG',"

He responded in Mandarin to Lisa, "This is why the Dong people are named such, DONG!!"

Because of the research and writing, I am doing on the Dong communities, I was completely taken with the bowl. He saw that I loved the "singing bowl," and offered it to me. I was, and am, so humbled to receive and now care for this beautiful Dong bell-sounding bowl with its single small shadowy figure painted on it. How does one begin to thank someone for the gift of a lifetime that has so much meaning?

We had our pictures taken together, and I know that bowl sounding like a bell is the inspiration for this book, as it is the bowl that holds the blessings described in these pages.

As I see this heaping bowl full of blessings, I ask myself what meaning does my soul crave? How can I really make a difference for others?

It seems there is really only one word that describes me, BRIDGE. I am a bridge between people, and between them and their success. Like the song I used to sing while my mom played our piano at home, "Lord, lead me, along the way. For if you lead me, I cannot stray. Lord let me walk this day with Thee, Lead me, oh Lord, lead me."

> "
> He saw that I loved the "singing bowl," and offered it to me.
> "

TEA AND CUPS

Boiling hot water, red tea, black tea, green tea, so many colors and flavors of tea from which to choose. While I am on this path talking about tea and cups, let me say, I have now learned from some dear Chinese friends how important tea, cups, the choice and time for tea are critical in Hunan. Linda, Lisa, and Mandy, have shared their joy of tea with me at meetings, in my hotel room, at the tea house and everywhere in between. There are certain rules about time together for tea. You need to make the first pot of boiling tea to pour in the tiny cups to sanitize, sterilize, or just plain clean the cups. Then leaves of the special tea(s) are placed in the in the strainer of the pot and hot water is poured over them. It drains through the leaves into the pot which then is tipped to pour into the tiny cup, which holds no more than three tablespoons of liquid at a time, and enjoyed by friends and colleagues who gather to enjoy each other's company or to make critical work decisions together. I realize I have given a very simplistic explanation of a very complex ceremony of making and drinking tea. It is an expression of liquid friendship.

"

…I have now learned from some dear Chinese friends how important tea, cups, the choice and time for tea are critical in Hunan.

"

THE WARM COAT

As the wind whips around the trees and blows the rain, the promise of winter is upon Huaihua. With that comes the change of clothing from short sleeved shirts with a light sweater to going to the back of one's stash of clothes and finding the warmest coat and hat in your possession. Hum, what if that stash of warm clothes is thousands of miles away buried in an entry way closet in Minnesota. That is where my warmest coat makes its home. Today I was shivering when I woke up. I certainly wished I would have brought a warmer coat to China, but the temperature had been 80 degrees which is 50 Celsius, when I boarded the plane and watched the 10,000 lakes of MN disappear beneath the clouds as we took off for Shanghai. Now that decision to bring only a light travel raincoat which has had trips to various countries seemed wise then, and a little crazy now. So, today after a nice lunch at a downtown steak place, the ladies set out to find a winter coat for me. I know that no matter what Psalms: 139 says about God knowing our form before we are born, I know he must not be surprised, but chuckling, as we went from store to store to store to store trying on nearly 50 beautiful Chinese coats on this non-dainty, non-Chinese frame. They were a little too narrow in the hips, or the shoulders, or too short in the sleeves, too short all over, or purple, or flowered, or the right color but the wrong design… what a lot of laughs as I felt like the Stepsister in the Cinderella story trying on the glass slipper… nothing fit during the nearly three hour journey from store and mall to mall, except one designer Chinese coat that was 30% off of 13,000 Yuan/RMB or $2033 USD, a little over this professor's budget. Then, we taxied over to another shopping area, walked into a store, and the first coat I tried on fit like it was made for me… I think this butterscotch colored warm and fuzzy coat is exactly the one God planted in that department store just for me. Isn't it interesting, the last one we find is always the best. Perhaps it is an analogy for the last thing we pursue, becomes the thing we have always dreamed about, but never thought would happen. Now, I have a butterscotch colored coat that makes me look like a teddy bear, but so warm and loved because my Chinese girlfriends cared for their very cold "American Mom".

> "
> Isn't it interesting, the last one we find is always the best. Perhaps it is an analogy for the last thing we pursue, becomes the thing we have always dreamed about, but never thought would happen.
> "

CHINESE VALUES A, B, C, D, AND IMPORTANTLY, E

While contemplating about how important it is for me to learn more about Han and Dong cultures, I realized I had the perfect opportunity to create a small study about what my students valued about their Chinese culture. With convenience sampling of 70 of my students in the Appreciating American Literature course at Huaihua University who were studying and speaking in English. I asked them the following question. What are the most important values which need to be preserved in Chinese culture?" I did not qualify if I were speaking of Han or one of the 56 minority groups in who call China home. It was a small research project, as I have only talked to the 70 Chinese students across a five week period asking them simply, "If you were to name values you have been taught, what word(s) would you use to name them in English?" Their answers fell into an easy pattern for me to remember them, the A, B, C's, including letters D and E.

A - Always be respectful (especially to your parents, the poor and disabled).
B - Be honest, and know right from wrong "bad".
C – Caring and kindness shown to all.
D – Discipline with love.
E - Emphasize education.

I find the students in my class, whom I have really gotten to know, generally live to match these values as they attend their classes and live their lives in the dormitory. I have found they respect their elders (in the way they speak about their parents), yet are emerging in their respect for those their own age, similarly to their USA age mates who are in my classes at Concordia University, St. Paul.

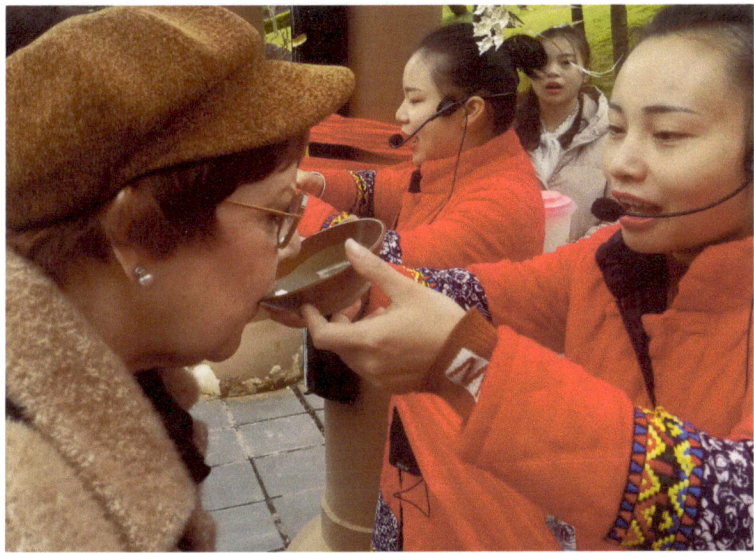

> "
> Their answers fell into an easy pattern for me to remember them, the A, B, C's, including letters D and E.
> "

TESTS AS PART OF GRADUATION

As my Chinese students wrap up their senior year and approach their competency tests, those who will teach English need to complete difficult tests to showcase their ability to teach in English. They need to perform before a judge who will rank them. Their anxiety is great, because they need to score well in order to qualify to go on for Master's Degrees. As they prepare for these tests, I have had the opportunity to have many meals in the canteen and chat with them about how to both prepare and to reduce their anxiety before they go for their tests. These experiences for them are much like the tests that students in the United States take prior to qualifying for teaching licenses…almost always causing a great deal of stress. Some of the stress helps to peak their performance, but it also can be a roadblock for students who are learning English and must use it for their examinations and competitions both locally in Huaihua and province-wide.

In my times of helping the students plan for their futures, I have shared *backwards mapping* and leadership strategies with them, because, as they plan for what's next, they need a strategy on which to focus. They often get caught in helping their colleagues also study and finish their group work. In doing so, they often shortcut their own study time. I appreciate their caring kindness, and also encouraged them to focus on their own goals, to use an image of aiming for a star as their "dream next step". Then, I have helped them determine all the steps they must take to reach that star. This is *backwards mapping*. At first *backwards mapping* seemed to be a difficult concept, until I suggested they visualize themselves standing on their star way up in the sky looking back to where they were at this very point, imagining what individual things they must do to reach their dream-star. That seemed to click, even across languages.

> "
> In my times of helping the students plan for their futures, I have shared *backwards mapping* and leadership strategies with them, because, as they plan for what's next, they need a strategy on which to focus.
> "

SLANT OF LIGHT

Author Emily Dickinson wrote a poem entitled "Slant of Light" as both appreciative of human nature and of the world in which human nature exists. She was a Transcendentalist, or at least admired Ralph Waldo Emerson and Henry David Thoreau who were identified as such. They were writing during the 1800's when people believed "the individual was at the center of the universe." And what, might you ask, would incline me to add this to my bowl of blessings. Well, here it is… while I have been in Huaihua, I have had the privilege of teaching the Appreciation of American Literature as a co-teacher with Dr. Zhang Ling, university vice president and lecturer. Emily Dickinson, Ralph Waldo Emerson, Walt Whitman, and Mark Twain have been the authors we have explored together with our class of 70 Class 5 and 6 students (juniors and seniors). It has been both a joy and privilege to teach literature again. I have not had this pleasure since I began my career as an English and Journalism teacher at Irondale High School, in Mounds View, MN. During my teaching of Emily Dickinson this time, I explored with our class how and why Emily Dickinson might have chosen to write about a slant of light. It seemed such appropriate topic as Huaihua City, home of Huaihua University, was changing seasons. As winter approached, there was less light and yet more need for curtains on classrooms to keep in the warmth and keep out the cold wind and rain. So, at our 8:00 a.m. class, there was often only a "slant of light" peeking in where the curtains barely came together. Therefore, it was a perfect opportunity for me to walk to the window and draw back the curtains a little, while I talked about how Dickinson, who stayed alone most of her life in a small room, without much opportunity to explore nature except the minimal part of nature she could see from her shaded window. One could clearly imagine why she wrote mostly sad, melancholy, and somber poems exploring lost love, death, and dying when she could see but a slant of light. The students told me they will always remember this poem, because I showed them what a slant of light might be like for them, and was for Emily Dickinson.

When I was a teenager and reading about Emily Dickinson as a student myself, I often wondered how she could sit alone in her room for years without any real connection to the world. Yet, could understand her love of reading and writing, because, I too, loved to sit in my room and read stacks of books and write and draw for hours. I remember my mother talking about how a slant of light that came in my bedroom window was the golden light of peace and how it overpowered darkness.

> **"**
>
> I remember my mother talking about how a slant of light that came in my bedroom window was the golden light of peace and how it overpowered darkness.
>
> **"**

SISTERS, BROTHERS, AND THE GOLDEN THREADS

I always wished for more sisters and a brothers to share things with. Perhaps that is why I so treasure my various groups of sisters and brothers who have become a treasured part of my life. A couple of examples: MN School Psychologists, especially Marilyn; P.E.O. sisters, like Judy; Horsepowered Reading colleagues, especially the creator Michele, and Nurtured Heart Approach® groups of like-mined individuals, who are focused on education for women and children, especially Sarah. This newer group of Huaihua sisters, is yet another large group of women who are also like-minded, focused on education in art, design, teaching, and translation. These very special friends will always be my heart and soul sisters, because we have shared working together across 6000+ miles together, focused on building the rain and wind bridges of collegiality across cultures, disciplines, time, and space. We are changing the pace in a changed place with a change of perspective because our commitment to work together to make, our peoples' lives more meaningful. We realize that success is gritty, sweaty, and takes time. Sometimes the hard work is not glamorous. We realize that sometimes you have to be released from something to be called to something else. We challenge ourselves with what are we being called to do, and what golden threads will we have to release to change the way we think and work.

There are not only strong sisters, but brothers also who have been called together to join in important work to together to develop experiences and grow programs which have the potential to provide international experiences for Chinese and American students to develop skills and relationships for the future. These golden threads of relationships are braided together into the tapestry of my life and securely knotted beneath and through my very being always there to keep me strongly attached to them, to our work, and many times to our shared faith and strength together.

In working with these new sisters and brothers, I feel especially called to continue to use the leadership model which I adopted over 15 years ago: to model the way, create a shared vision, challenge things which are not satisfactorily moving forward, enable others to share their gifts and talents, and in every situation to encourage the hearts of all with whom I live, work, and play.

> "
>
> We are changing the pace in a changed place with a change of perspective because our commitment to work together to make, our peoples' lives more meaningful.
>
> "

GIFTS, GIFTS, GIFTS

Celebrations of successes and friendship are such a part of Huaihua, and perhaps the most visual recognition of the deep commitment we have to one another are the gifts we share with each other. There are gifts of flowers and fruit for welcome, and more flowers as gifts to celebrate good work, gifts of cake and cupcakes from *Made for You Bakery* for birthdays, hostess gifts of tea and more flowers, gifts of silver between special friends, gifts of praise, and gifts in times of sadness, too, at the death of a parent, friend, or child. Flowers and fruit are always appropriate and in season in Huaihua.

> "
> Flowers and fruit are always appropriate and in season in Huaihua.
> "

CELEBRATIONS

This year Concordia University, St. Paul, my university for 17 years, celebrates 125 years of "Living in Legacy," preparing church workers and teachers initially, and now preparing students for a myriad of professions where they can live out the mission "to prepare students for thoughtful and informed living, for dedicated service to God and humanity, for enlightened care of God's creation, all within the context of the Christian Gospel."

And my adopted university Huaihua University, celebrates 60 years this year. It was established in 1958. Huaihua University is a public higher education institution located in the small city of Huaihua (population range of 250,000-499,999 inhabitants), Hunan. Officially accredited and/or recognized by the Department of Education, Hunan Province, Huaihua University (HHU) as a large coeducational higher education institution. Huaihua University (HHU) offers courses and programs leading to officially recognized higher education degrees in several areas of study.

Both universities have had big celebrations. My special privilege was to present to President Song of Huaihua University a golden plaque from Concordia University, St. Paul, with good wishes and congratulations for 60 years of preparation of students and future opportunities to work together in international friendship. Yet, that was such a small part of the celebration and preparation for the special day of October 20, 2018. When thousands of people gathered in the pouring rain, to sit in heavy winter coats under plastic raincoats on the university playground to watch carefully prepared speeches and hundreds of students in musical and dramatic presentations marking the local history of both Han and minority populations. The singing, dancing and speaking were performed as if it were a bright and sunny day, instead of cold, wet, and windy. The costumes were so expertly designed, crafted, and worn by all the participants. The total presentation was nearly four hours long and from my vantage point, in the rows set aside for guests, it looked much like a gorgeous water-colored painting.

> "
>
> Living in legacy, both universities celebrate decades of service to their communities.
>
> "

FREEDOM FROM POVERTY: EMBROIDERY

Dong minority groups are flourishing in such cities of Jiangsu, Guangdong, Zhejiang, Fujian, Shanghai, and Beijing, yet in the 31 villages in the mountains there is significant poverty. The young adults in their late teens and early 20's are leaving the villages behind to find work in the cities. This situation abandons the elders, the sick, and disabled, leaving them alone in the villages to somehow get by without the joyful and supportive interactions with the youth and middle age families. As these elders walk about or merely sit, they are wearing the decorative Dong clothing reflecting the days of the past. Their clothes are decorated with gorgeous designs of dancing children, fish bones, sunflowers, birds, water, and mountains

Huaihua University and other universities are focused on sustaining this art of embroidery and intangible cultural heritage through their Art and Design Schools and teachers such as Silvia, Goldie, QQ, Alicia, Mandy, Amy, Lisa, Daniel, David, and Tim who are designing handbags, traditional and current fashion clothing, and jewelry inlaid into Miao and Sterling Silver. This is a new focus to market these products, earning funds to end the deep poverty of the Dong people in the mountains of Hunan.

"

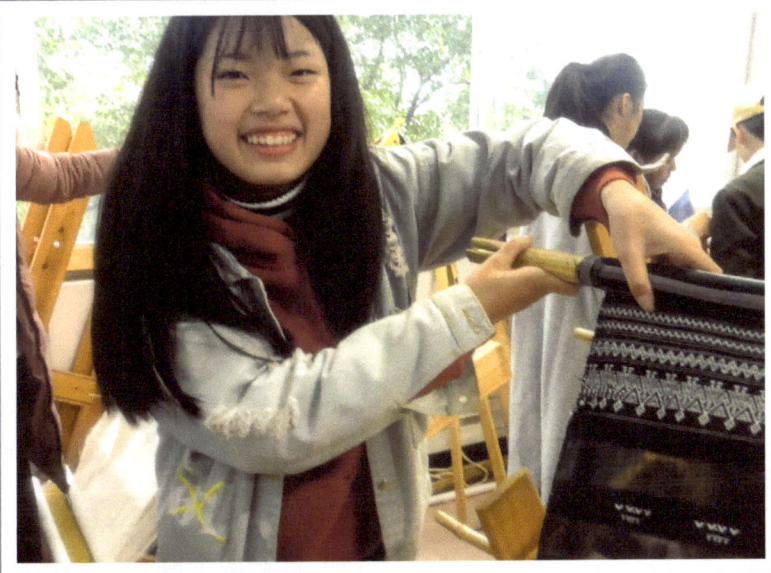

Huaihua University and other universities are focused on sustaining this art of embroidery and intangible cultural heritage…

"

PRESERVATION OF INTANGIBLE CULTURE

Huaihua University acquired a grant to build a cadre of weavers, for creating sustainability and preservation of intangible cultural heritage among the Dong people. As part of that plan, 40 youth from vocational schools were invited to the campus for one month to learn the very technical skill of weaving Dong cultural designs. I had the rare privilege to meet these young people from middle schools through high school graduates who labored many hours a day for a whole month to learn the designs. Each young person chose their design and worked with their vocational and Huaihua teachers to master the design weaving. I was with them only five times during the month, but was completely mystified at their excellent weaving and the great attitudes of the students as they sat at their brocade looms with thread and a 12 meter long woven shuttle carefully drawing the threads through one by one over and under the single threads to create the designs which emerged after many focused hours at the looms.

The process was exacting. Many pictures recorded their work and teachers and faculty visitors provided encouragement. The students welcomed the cheers and support giving them the confidence and hope to replicate the intricate historical designs. I so enjoyed watching the progress they made in capturing the perfect inspirational designs.

It has also allowed community teachers to bond with University personnel, as they created the patterns on paper, and taught in tandem in a co-teaching framework. Students were not in competition, but in a creative work space with many looms within arm's reach of each other so conversations, music, and the latest news from their cell phones could be shared.

Vocational students found their time in Huaihua to be a great opportunity to be on the college campus, to eat in the canteen, live in the dormitory, and to walk about the campus, enjoying the newly erected gate, and observe the flowers and trees which were planted for the 60th Year Anniversary of the University.

At the end of the month, these students returned to their villages or towns with new-found skills and a total sense of accomplishment. The plan is that they will continue to build their skills.

湖南文化遗产翻译与传播基地

Center for Hunan Cultural Heritage and Translation

An Institute Dedicated to the Preservation
and Development of Hunan's Diverse Ethnic
Communities to Be Shared With the Global
Community

"

As part of that plan, 40 youth
from vocational schools were
invited to the campus for
one month to learn the very
technical skill of weaving Dong
cultural designs.

"

THE HIGH SPEED TRAIN

Silvia, her son Landon, Queenie, and I took a trip to Chongqing from Huaihua by way of Guiyang on the bullet train snuggled into our seats. Riding on the high speed train is such a unique experience. I am reminded of Ezra Pounds poem about being on the Metro, seeing the faces through the rain and dirt soaked and streaky windows; where the faces of the people look like the colorful petals of spring flowers.

Of course taking pictures through the windows when the train is speeding along at 290 kilometers per hour is difficult, first because the man next to me kept rousing from his snoring sleep, and the pouring rain made my phone's camera nearly impossible to focus. So I took pictures in my mind's eye of the glorious mountains, valleys, and streams rushing by. This night the train is a busy place as the ladies who work on the train are cleaning the floor. They are dressed in purple dresses with aprons which hold their cleaning tools and their walkie-talkies. Everything to make for instant communication is secured to their waists, while their apron strings are tied securely in a bow. They remind me of the clean air truck in Huaihua, as they hum a little song as they work, just as the clean air truck plays its repeating song *It's a small world after all.*

The children are hopping and skipping up and down the narrow aisles, busy making friends with other children, as the food seller pushes her cart, dodging them. She is in a hurry to feed sandwiches, sushi, and sugary treats to the hungry passengers. Landon and his new friend, both six-year-olds were having so much fun eating their snacks and talking to all the people as they ran up and down the aisle.

It is Friday evening, with the weekend ahead, so many people were heading to Chongqing, such a huge city with 7.9 million people, bigger than Minneapolis and St. Paul, MN together. People are talking about the famed dish in this city- HOT POT. As I listen, I am remembering conversations about using chopsticks when I first arrived in China, when I had no knowledge of the technique for managing the very small bites of food, helping myself to the bitty little portions, and being encouraged to practice picking up roasted peanuts with chopsticks to practice my skills to avoid being teased about my awkward skills.

A wiggly little boy, barely 18 months old was sitting just ahead of us. He was a little fussy one until his mom gave him her phone. By himself, he found a game and was contented for the next hour playing one game after another. Phones can be such a soothing toy. It's a good thing there was a USB charger by their seat on the train, so his mom could recharge her battery.

As the hours passed by, these sounds of the train became so soothing. the clicking of computer games, soft sounds of sleeping passengers, the wheels of the food carts, brooms sweeping up crumbs, tears of a hungry baby, the laughter of the boys full of energy, quiet Mandarin voices of parents singing their little ones to sleep, the snoring of men tired from their weeks' work, the subtle sound of someone's movie playing on their phone, and a pickup game being played by two little friends. The train paused at a village and a young college student rushed off at the stop to embrace her waiting friend

The train began again, the trip toward another town, while the clicking sound of a man doing his calculations on an old-fashioned spread sheet, the train cleaner calling for trash as she tugged the plastic bag down the walkway and over the playing children in her way, yet not fussing at them, but carefully stepping over them, and then a restlessness. Passengers were shuffling their feet, gathering their things, and calling home on their cell phones as the conductor calls out the next station. People seemed more anxious, obviously knowing was nearly time to wrestle their bags again and head toward their next destination.

"

At 290 kilometers per hour seeing the faces through the rain and dirt soaked and streaky windows; where the faces of the people look like the colorful petals of spring flowers.

"

CHONGQING

As mentioned, Chongqing is known for spicy food, and especially for hot pot. After our things were settled in the hotel, we sought the infamous hot pot at a nearby restaurant. In this case, the hot pot itself was a large divided stainless steel bowl about 15 inches across. One side of the bowl had oil with hot red peppers floating in it, and the other side contained both. You choose what you want to cook, and we had pork, goose, squid, quail eggs, shrimp balls, mushrooms, lettuce, celery, and some other greens. We made our own sauces to have on the side with cilantro, peppers, soy sauce, fish sauce, and a few indescribable herbs. Rice or noodles were offered, but we didn't have any. What a feast as we put foods in to cook and helped ourselves with our chopsticks; however, often I was served my food, as it is honoring to have someone serve you as a guest. What a hot, spicy, and delicious meal!

We were stuffed when we finished all the special foods. It seemed very important to take a walk along the Yanze River after we ate, because we were so satisfied, yet full of the delicious food. What an experience seeing the beautiful colored lights outlining every downtown building and the new bridge. There were hundreds of people walking, weaving through the crowds to go down to the caves or walk on the bridge crossing the river. A cacophony of sounds penetrated the atmosphere there: tooting cars (those are everywhere in China), trains, boat horns, people celebrating together at outdoor cafes, taxis and DD cars (like Uber) zooming by and then jamming on their brakes when drivers see their contracted riders appearing on the street corners or at the side of the street. Sometimes people are waiting among the muddy footprints. Sometimes riders just pop out of the crowd. When it is your turn, you hop into the car. Even though you have prearranged your destination, you really never know where you will be dropped off, sometimes at the hotel or sometimes at the side of the freeway, and you have to climb over the barricade or railing… what unexpected experiences.

"

Hot pot … and a cacophony of sounds penetrated the atmosphere there.

"

ORANGES

In the fall in Southern China, you can hardly pass a fruit stand without the sweet scent of oranges overtaking every other fragrance. You must not just go to a fruit market for your oranges, but take a few hours to go the orchard and pick boxes of oranges yourself with your electrical wire cutters to snip the orange from the branches. Thankfully Mr. Zhou drove his big Jeep, and Amy, Tim, Goldie, Mandy, Cherry, and I made the trip to the orchard where we met Mr. Lor the owner of the orchard who helped us know to pick the reddest orange fruit facing he sun, not the yellow or light orange fruit hiding among the lower leaves and branches. It is very important to cut the oranges from the stem without pricking the skin of the orange or it will leak juice and/or mold before you can eat it. Many of the oranges actually were sagging from the branches because they were so full of sweet sticky juice. Mr. Lor gave us extra boxes of oranges which were a welcome addition to our own big boxes of delicious, fragrant Hunan oranges. I now understand why American oranges are called *sun-kissed*, because without the sun… no sweetness! A word to the wise, be sure to wash your hands and clothes right away when you come home, so you don't get itchy from the orange tree sap.

> "
>
> It is very important to cut the oranges from the stem without pricking the skin of the orange or it will leak juice and/or mold before you can eat it.
>
> "

SADNESS

At times when we are away from our home routine, friends, and loved ones, a sadness comes upon our circumstances. Our bowl of blessings no matter how full has one fewer person sharing their blessings this side of heaven. For me, while I was in China, we lost our dear elder grandma, Nao's mom. Our Hmong Culture and Language Program will not be the same without her helping us garden, make *paj ntaub* (an embroidered story cloth) or re-tying our sashes on the day of our Camp Community Celebration. Her sweet spirit has always been a special blessing to us all.

We are here for only a moment, visitors and strangers in a land as our ancestors were before us. Our days on earth are like a passing shadow, gone so soon, without a trace, and the things here on earth and in heaven are merely changed to the will of God's hand, yet God tugs us to heaven like a kite that flies out of a child's hand as he takes us to be with him.

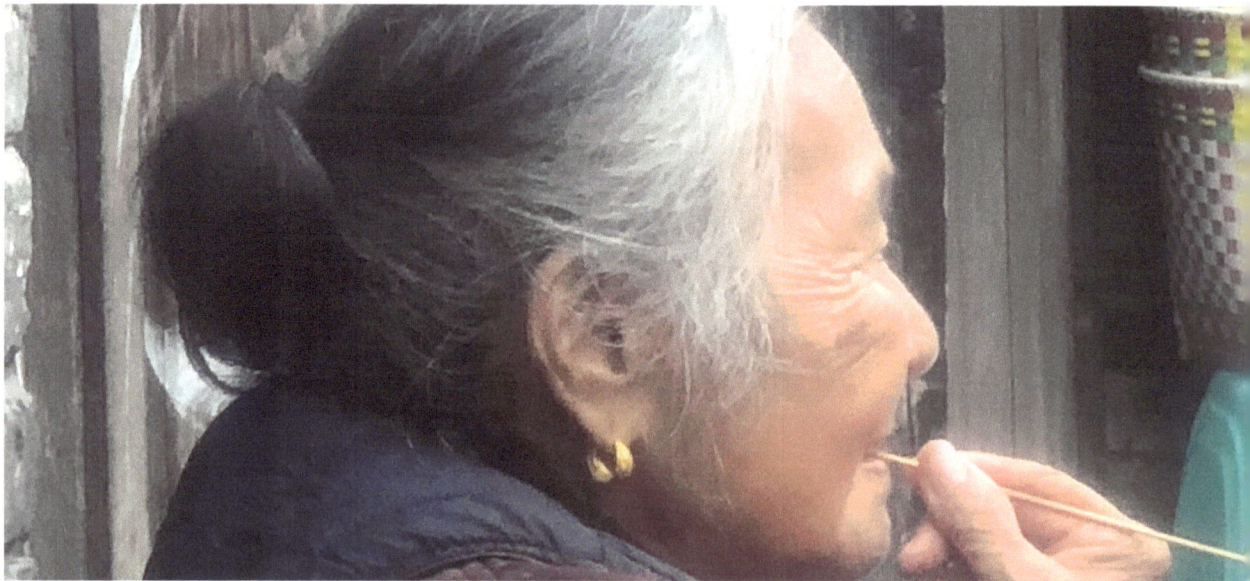

"

things here on earth and in
heaven are merely changed to
the will of God's hand, yet God
tugs us to heaven like a kite that
flies out of a child's hand

"

UNEXPECTED FIND

As we wandered down a small village street, eating chestnuts, walnuts, and oranges, we came upon a small stately white painted church with Pope Francis's picture hanging on a fence nearby. I didn't expect to find a church in that small town. Later on, as we approached a beautiful bridge, seated at the edge of the bridge were several onlookers and a small musical group, with a woman playing the two string violin, a gentleman playing a wooden flute and another gentleman playing am electric organ. As we walked across a bridge, we were greeted by a woman singing a very lilting song quickly joined by one of our colleagues, Amy, to sing a very special Chinese song… so unexpected, and so lovely.

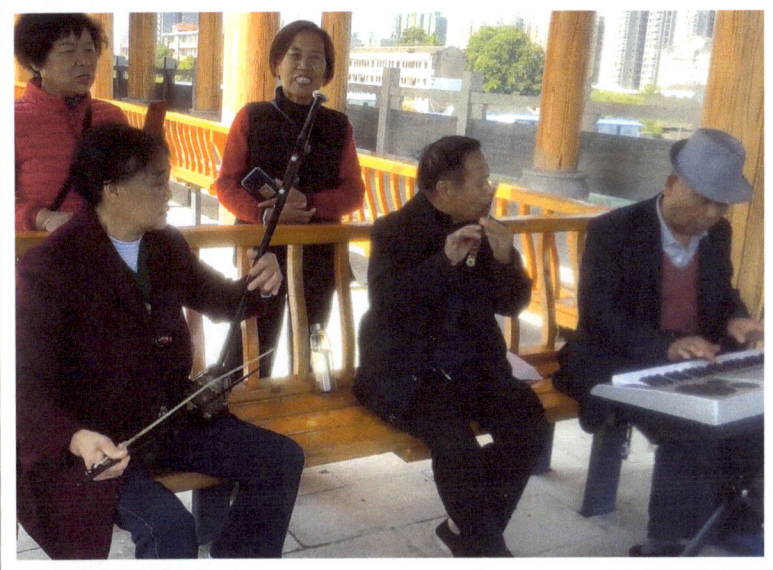

At the edge of the bridge were several onlookers and a small musical group, with a woman playing the two string violin, a gentleman playing a wooden flute and another playing an electric organ.

PAUSE AND REFLECTION

No internet connection. No Facebook, No Google Scholar. No sunshine… a time of pause. There are times in one's life that there is a PAUSE… a time to reflect on what have we been called to do, by whom, and for whom. As I have written this book, I have re-read my daily journal from a time of pause, work, and reflection. I am grateful for the people who have also been on this path with me, my dear husband, Jim, our children and their families (Mandy and Matt, Silas and Gretel, Brad and wife Cris, and four-legged Loki.

I am so grateful to the Concordia University Regents, President Ries, Dr. Marilyn Reineck, Vice President for Academic Affairs; Dr. Kevin Hall, Dean, College of Business and Technology; Professor Lonn David Maly, Dean, College of Education; Dr. Katie Fischer, and Dean, College of Health and Science.

My concluding contemplation is this: Thank you, Lord for loving me and my family around the world. I am grateful for this sabbatical time of PAUSE and REFLECTION. I now understand more about why you withdrew from the hills to talk with your Father. Please, Lord, help me continue your work, your path ordained just for me. Please protect all my family at home, in China, and in the other countries I have been blessed to visit this year of my sabbatical, at the invitation of Secretaries of Education, Parliament, and the International Association of School Psychologists to Romania, Japan, Poland, and China. Give us all clean hearts full of your peace and the recognition that there is none like You.

I have put this verse from Genesis 12:1-2 (NIV) in my heart "Go from your country, your people, and your father's household to the land I will show you… I will bless you… and you will be a blessing."

I trust I have been, and will be, a blessing always, to those on my path building bridges with the golden threads of relationships wound through, and enjoying the bowl full of blessing as I journey on in my life, one faith step at a time, remembering *where though art, that, is home.*

I will keep in mind the Chinese proverb: the method for a good life is to have a clean heart full of peace.

> **"**
>
> Thank you, Lord for loving me and my family around the world. I am grateful for this sabbatical time of PAUSE and REFLECTION.
>
> **"**

www.ingramcontent.com/pod-product-compliance
Lightning Source LLC
Chambersburg PA
CBHW042003100426
42813CB00020B/2963